· Oxford Scientific Films ·

MOUNTAIN WILDLIFE

Ben Osborne

MALLARD
PRESS

MALLARD PRESS
An Imprint of BDD Promotional Book Company, Inc.,
666 Fifth Avenue, New York, NY 10103.

Mallard Press and its accompanying design and logo
are trademarks of BDD Promotional Book Company, Inc.

CLB 2335
Copyright © 1989 Colour Library Books Ltd.
© 1989 Illustrations: Oxford Scientific Films Ltd,
Long Hanborough, England.
Color separation by Hong Kong Graphic Arts Ltd, Hong Kong.
First published in the United States of America
in 1989 by The Mallard Press.
Printed and bound in Italy by Fratelli Spada, SpA.
All rights reserved.
ISBN 0 792 45024 8

Contents

These pages: Mount McKinley provides a spectacular backcloth for these mountain goat ewes and lambs.

Previous page: young male ibex play-fighting on a narrow ledge in the French Alps.

1
Mountains

Mountains are the world's high places. They tower above the forests and plains, and provide some of the most hostile *environments* for wildlife on the earth's surface.

Some mountain summits are only 3,000 feet above sea level, while others rise to 24,000 feet. However, we call them both mountains because a mountain is defined by its relationship to the surrounding land.

In Scotland, for example, where much of the land is near to sea level, a summit of only 3,000 feet is a significant height above the average land height and is, therefore, called a mountain. In Tibet most of the land is a flat plateau at an *altitude* of around 15,000 feet. Despite its height, this plateau is not a mountain. The true mountains in this region are the high peaks that rise to over 18,000 feet around the edge of the plateau.

Some mountains are produced by volcanic activity. Where a fracture occurs in the earth's crust, molten lava can be forced outward, cooling as it reaches the surface. The build up of rock can be great enough to form large mountains. The recent eruption of Mount St. Helens in the state of Washington is an example of this kind of mountain building. Mountains are also formed by a folding of the earth's surface. The earth is covered by a relatively thin skin called the crust, which is divided into sections or plates. When two plates of the crust are forced together they crumple and fold, creating unevenness in the landscape. This "tectonic" activity has produced many of the great *mountain ranges* of the world, such as the Himalayas and the Alps.

A Rocky Mountain goat poses on an airy stance in the Rocky Mountains.

Nun Kun, 23,787 feet high, towers above the Suru River in the western Himalayas.

Dramatic rock spires characterize the mountains of the southern Andes in Torres del Paine National Park.

Mountains occur in most countries – from the equator to the poles. The Rockies in North America, the Andes in South America and the Himalayas in Asia are three of the largest mountain ranges on earth. All of them stretch for over 1,000 miles and pass through many different countries. They also provide a wide range of *habitats*. The Rockies are clad extensively in pine forests, with alpine meadows above the *tree line* culminating in exposed, rocky peaks. The Himalayas, however, contain a much broader variety of habitats, from the deserts of the Ladakh uplands to the dense rainforests of Assam.

Animals have invaded most mountain habitats, although the severe conditions found on upper slopes rule out all but the hardiest species. Nevertheless, there is a sufficient variety of habitats to accommodate a range of species. These form a number of simple *food chains*. For example, in certain mountain ranges larger grazing animals, like wild sheep, goats and deer, are preyed upon by major *carnivores*, including the mountain lion and snow leopard, while smaller predators, especially the birds of prey, rely on the numerous pikas, lemmings and small songbirds to make up their diet.

2

Mountain Habitats

Mountains provide many different habitats in which animals can live. Generally, as you get further from the equator and as you get higher above sea level, the conditions become less favorable, making it more difficult for animals and plants to survive. Not only are mountains cold and windy, but they can have poor soils, low atmospheric concentrations of oxygen and carbon dioxide, and high ultra-violet radiation.

There is no such thing as a "typical" mountain, but we shall invent one to illustrate the arrangement of habitats that can be found on mountains. At the top of our "typical" mountain is a rocky summit. On one side of the peak there are huge cliffs interspersed with ledges and pinnacles. On the other side is a glacier, a white river of ice which pours slowly down the mountain, creaking and groaning as it passes over bumps in the underlying rock. On steeper ground the glacier cracks, forming *crevasses* in the surface of the ice. Around the glacier lies an area of scree – rubble that is formed when frost shatters the bedrock. There is little soil on the scree and new boulders frequently crash down from the cliffs above, so it is a difficult environment in which to survive.

A small stream of meltwater trickles from the glacier. Cold and clear, the water splashes down over the boulders, carving a little passage through the rocks. Eventually it collects in a dip in the valley below to form a small mountain lake, an important source of drinking water for migrant birds or for the wild sheep and goats that visit these high regions.

Below the screes and the lake lie the alpine meadows. Although the growing season is short at these high altitudes, the meadows support many beautiful wild flowers and can be very colorful, especially in early summer. The meadows provide grazing for large *herbivores*, as well as smaller animals like marmots and ground squirrels. They also provide ground cover for insects and the few reptiles that feed on them.

The lower slopes of the mountain are covered with forests. Trees are sensitive to climate and can only tolerate a certain amount of cold. Trees at the highest altitudes (juniper and birch) are gnarled and stunted, while lower down, out of the wind and frost, there are tall, straight pines. Lower still there are deciduous woodlands, and then the forest meets the jungle which dominates the valleys below.

Not all mountains provide such a variety of habitats. In Antarctica, for example, the mountains are covered in ice, with only a few rocky peaks showing through the glaciers. In Borneo, which is on the equator and therefore much warmer, the mountains are completely covered in tropical rainforest.

Above: marmots often site their burrows on exposed knolls from which they have a commanding view of the surrounding terrain.

Facing page top: alpine meadows provide grazing and shelter for many small mammals.

Facing page bottom: deer climb to the alpine meadows to graze during the summer.

3
Mountain Flowers

Plants that live on mountains have to withstand a range of extreme weather conditions. They must also resist being eaten by herds of both wild and domestic *herbivores*.

Lack of water is one of the main problems facing plants that live in the alpine meadows and other areas above the tree line. Not only is rainfall low, but the soil is often poor and the slopes are steep, so water drains away rapidly. To counteract this, many mountain plants are succulents, which means that their leaves are spongy and can hold reserves of water. This water can be used in times of drought and is replenished when the rain comes. Hairy stems and leaves also help plants to conserve moisture by lessening the drying effects of the wind. Other species put out extensive root systems which give them a greater ability to collect what water is available. On the high, rocky peaks only lichens can survive the extreme cold and lack of water.

Above: gentians are one of the typical plants found on alpine meadows in many mountain regions.

Right: to avoid grazing animals, many mountain plants grow on inaccessible ledges.

Most alpine plants are low and slow-growing. Being tall is a disadvantage in an environment where gale-force winds blast down from the high peaks and flatten anything over a few inches high. Except during the short summer season, when conditions are temporarily favorable, there is little option for mountain plants but to grow slowly. And in winter, when a covering of snow blocks out the sunlight and maintains a sub-zero temperature, they lie *dormant*.

When the snow melts in the spring, the hot sunshine heats the soil and the combination of warmth and light stimulates a rapid response

Because they produce fresh growth in the summer, alpine plants attract the attention of herds of grazing animals: sheep, goats and deer roam the alpine meadows throughout the summer.

The plants have evolved a number of defenses against grazing animals: some grow spines, others sting, while a few have developed a pungent aroma which animals find unpleasant. The ultimate defense is for the plant to avoid contact altogether by growing where it can't be grazed. However, there are very few places, even on the steepest cliffs, that the agile ibex

Above: prolific vegetation clothes the slopes of the Ruwenzori Mountains in Africa.

Facing page: alpine meadows are carpeted with wild flowers during the summer.

Mountain plants tend to be stunted and slow-growing, like this house-leek.

from the plants. Within a few days the ground will be carpeted with crocuses, and these are followed by a colorful profusion of other flowers. Deep blue gentians, bright yellow buttercups, pale yellow poppies, flamboyant orange lilies, purple orchids and many others paint the alpine meadows with a stunning explosion of color during the height of summer.

cannot reach. And if a plant does start to grow on an inaccessible cliff ledge, it still has to find enough water and nutrients to support its growth, so this is not necessarily an easy option.

Below the tree line conditions are much more favorable for plant survival: not only do the trees create their own shelter, but their extensive roots prevent soil erosion. Water does not drain away so quickly from these slopes and, because woodlands are found on the lower slopes of the mountain, the temperatures are higher. This combination of warmer, wetter conditions allows the growth of many plants which would not survive in the exposed alpine meadows.

4
Survival in the Mountains

To survive in the mountains animals must be able to cope with some of the severest weather in the world, they have to be able to find enough food, and they have to avoid being eaten.

To withstand the cold, most mountain animals have developed a thick coat. In many cases this consists of a fleecy inner layer of warm hair which retains heat, and a coarse outer layer which protects the animal from wind and rain.

The vicuna of South America has an extremely warm coat, which allows it to survive the savagely cold winters of the high Andes. In summer, however, the hot sunshine can create comparatively mild conditions. The vicuna has a bare patch of skin on its inner thigh through which it loses heat by standing with its legs apart. When it has cooled sufficiently, it brings its legs together to prevent further heat loss.

The ultimate fur coat is found on the snow leopard, a medium-sized mountain cat which inhabits the high peaks of the Himalayas. This beautiful animal has a remarkably thick coat of smoky gray fur patterned with darker gray "rosettes". This coloration makes the snow leopard extremely difficult to see, whether it is on rocky ground or on snow.

The snow leopard illustrates two other important adaptations: it has larger feet than other cats of its size, and it has a long tail. Both these features are useful to an animal that has to travel in deep snow. The large feet act rather like snowshoes, preventing the snow leopard from sinking into deep snow, while the tail balances the animal when it is running down unstable snow slopes.

Most mountain mammals live on steep, rocky ground. The animals best suited for this life style have developed special feet which provide a good grip. The hoof of the Rocky Mountain goat has a hard edge and a treaded sole which gives it good friction. The chamois and the llama have flexible, elastic pads on the base of their hooves that grip on to the roughness of the rock. Some animals, rather than face up to the rigors of the mountain environment, escape when the going gets tough. Small rodents, for example, escape the harsh winter by burrowing into the soil and hibernating until the weather improves. Many species of deer only use the high pastures in summer, preferring to shelter on the low ground

---

To maintain camouflage, some mountain animals, such as the willow ptarmigan turn white in winter.

when the snow comes. Small songbirds only visit the mountains to breed during the short summer

Color is important to many small mammals and birds. The few that do remain in the mountains all year round change color in the winter to become less conspicuous as they feed in the snow. The ptarmigan goes white, as does the mountain hare, though both revert to their more usual brown color in the spring.

Alpine salamanders, which lack the protection afforded by a covering of fur, have evolved a black pigmentation. This absorbs the high levels of ultraviolet radiation that are common to mountain environments and also enhances the reptile's ability to absorb heat. Like the salamander, many mountain species are darker than their lowland counterparts.

Top: because of the cold, windy conditions often experienced on mountains, most mountain mammals have a long, thick coat.
Above: alpine salamanders have black pigmentation which absorbs ultraviolet light and heat.

5
Mountain Sheep

Wild sheep are found in many of the world's mountain ranges and are much larger animals than the more familiar domestic variety. There are several types of wild sheep. Argali, Marco Polo sheep and American bighorn sheep are large animals, some the size of a small pony. The males have enormous, tightly-curled *horns*, up to three feet long. Urials, mouflon and thinhorn or Dall sheep are much smaller and have less substantial horns.

The male sheep use their horns for fighting. During the breeding season, the *rams* join the ewes and fight each other to decide who is going to mate with the females. Fighting is a test of strength, size and stamina. The rams rear up on their hind legs and butt each other, clashing their horns with a terrific bang.

Bighorn sheep are found in the northern Rocky Mountains, while argali and Marco Polo sheep roam the high, arid plains of Central Asia in search of grazing. As the vegetation is often sparse in these areas, they have to travel long distances to find enough to eat. Outside the breeding season males and females usually form separate herds.

The smaller sheep species are more agile than the bighorns, an adaptation which allows them to use steeper ground. They are often found near cliffs, and may climb steep crags to avoid predators.

Rocky Mountain sheep head-butting during a fight.

The mouflon was originally found throughout the mountains of southern and central Europe, though it was exterminated from most of its range by excessive hunting. Small populations survived in the remote mountain strongholds of Corsica and Sardinia. Animals from these populations have been transplanted back onto mainland Europe, where their numbers are now slowly recovering.

Excessive hunting, both for their meat and for their horns, is a problem for many wild sheep, and the populations of some species are at dangerously low levels. In many areas there is the added pressure of grazing *competition* from flocks of domestic sheep, which use the same pastures as wild sheep, thus reducing the amount of food that is available.

Left: male bighorn sheep bear enormous curled horns with which they fight during the breeding season.

Below: Dall sheep lambs search for grazing in the alpine meadows of Denali National Park in Alaska.

6
Wild Goats

Goats have adapted superbly to living in mountains. They can survive in severe weather, are superb climbers, and can feed on the coarsest vegetation. They differ from sheep in a number of ways. Their horns are straighter, they have a pungent body odor and the males have beards. Goats also have flatter, longer tails.

The ibex is the most widespread species of goat, and is found throughout the mountains of Asia, Europe and North Africa. It has a fine sense of balance and can be seen leaping effortlessly along narrow ledges and clattering down fearsome precipices. During the *rut*, the males fight spectacular battles, clashing their long, curved horns and butting into each other as they try to maintain a foothold on a rocky slab. Females, and even the tiniest of *kids*, also show a natural poise in this near-vertical world.

Like other goats, ibex eat practically anything, though they tend to avoid the spiny and bitter-tasting plants. In winter they stay at high altitudes and have to survive the worst of the weather. When there is a heavy snow cover they have to remember the good feeding areas so that they can dig through the snow to find food. They also browse on bushes which stick up through the snow.

In the daytime, ibex feed on the gentler slopes but retire at night to steep cliffs to avoid predators. Each winter many of them are swept away by avalanches which pour down from the high peaks.

Two hundred years ago ibex were virtually extinct in Europe as a result of relentless hunting during the previous few centuries. In 1854 the Italians successfully established a herd of ibex in Gran Paradiso National Park. By 1879, the population had reached 600 animals. The Swiss, hoping to follow the Italian example, set up a national park in the Alps, assuming that the Italians would sell them a few of their ibex. The Italians refused this request so the Swiss crossed the border, captured some ibex and smuggled them back to Switzerland. Realizing that this

tactic might be repeated, the Italians then agreed to sell additional ibex to the Swiss and a viable population was established in Switzerland. Since then, other reintroductions have taken place and the European ibex population is gradually recovering.

Above: Rocky Mountain goats browse on sparse vegetation on steep cliffs.

Facing page top: a female chamois digs through the snow to graze on an alpine meadow in the Abruzzi Alps.

Facing page bottom: mountain goats are completely at home in a steep, rocky environment from birth.

The Rocky Mountain goat has spread throughout the mountains of the western United States and Canada. Unlike the ibex, these handsome animals often descend to low altitudes in winter, occasionally to near sea level in particularly harsh winters. This behavior is more characteristic of deer, which are not as well-adapted to the mountains as goats or sheep.

7
Deer

Deer are less hardy than wild sheep and goats. Most species prefer to live in forests rather than on the high pastures, though they visit the alpine meadows in summer when there is plenty of grazing and the weather is warm. Reindeer are the hardiest species, seeking shelter in the forests only in the very coldest conditions. At other times they live on open *tundra* moorland, surviving on a diet of lichens and grasses.

The red deer, like its close relative the wapiti in America, has successfully invaded many mountain areas. Even on the wet, windswept moors of the Scottish Highlands, red deer have survived with little shelter and poor grazing. The effects of this poor environment are, however, obvious when these herds are compared with red deer from the heavily forested mountains of Germany and Sweden. Scottish red deer have stunted body growth, poorer *antlers*, lighter body weights, higher mortality and fewer calves than their Continental counterparts.

Above: a red deer stag. This species has colonized many mountain ranges throughout the world.

Top: a bull wapiti caught in a snow storm, Yellowstone National Park, USA.

Red deer have been introduced to mountainous areas of New Zealand and South America, where they have bred successfully but upset the natural balance of wildlife. In New Zealand they have destroyed large areas of forest by over-grazing, and in South America they have taken over from the native pudu and Andean deer.

The roe deer, a small species with a rich brown coat and a white rump patch, is one of the most attractive mountain deer. While red deer

---

The diminutive roe deer is a solitary species, preferring the woodland margins to more open meadows.

form harems during the rut and one male will mate with several females, roe deer are *monogamous*. They pair for life, and live within a defended territory that includes patches of woodland interspersed with clearings.

Small deer are very secretive, none more so than the musk deer which lives in the high birch and rhododendron thickets of the Himalayas. These hardy animals remain at high altitudes during the winter, scraping lichens and mosses off tree trunks when other grazing is covered in snow. The males have a special *gland* which contains musk, a compound which is used medicinally throughout Asia. As musk is very valuable, poachers have shot so many of these deer that they are now seriously endangered.

8
Mammals Under Ground

The ultimate way to avoid the winter is to *burrow* down into the ground and sleep from autumn to spring. Most of the mountain-dwelling rodents do just this, though there are occasional exceptions – even a house mouse may be seen scurrying around on a cold January morning at 14,000 feet in the Himalayas. This tiny animal somehow manages to cope with a temperature of 1.5°F.

Marmots are one of the most obvious rodents living in the mountains of Europe, Asia and North America. Even if they can't be seen, their shrill whistles usually disturb the peace of the alpine meadows. Marmots live in colonies where they like to have a good view, as they are always on the lookout for predators. Marmots have numerous enemies – wolves, foxes, snow leopards, mountain lions, man – so they are wary and difficult to approach. In certain parts of the Rockies and the Alps, however, they have gotten used to man's presence and are often bold enough to beg for food from tourists.

Rodents which *hibernate* must make good use of the plentiful food available in the summer. Much of their time is spent eating, though they can also be seen sunning themselves on rocks, especially in the middle of the day. By the autumn they are enormously fat and will be able to survive without eating for six or seven months.

Young marmots hide under a boulder.

A hibernating chipmunk.

As the temperatures start to fall, marmots can be seen waddling around gathering bunches of dry grass which they use to line their burrows. When they finally decide that it is time to sleep, they seal themselves in their burrows by blocking up the entrance with earth and grass.

Although they live in burrows and store food for the winter, pikas do not hibernate. These small, mouse-like animals are active throughout the winter, when they make extensive runways under the snow through which they can reach *caches* of food. Their diet includes a wide range of plants, which are dried in the sun before being stored underground for use in the winter.

Like pikas, lemmings spend much of the year in tunnels under the snow. These stout little rodents, about the size of a small rat, spend the summer scurrying around among the dense mats of lichen and moss that are typically found on the tundra. They remain on the high ground during the winter. The young are reared in nests of soft plant material. If the winter is short and the weather is comparatively mild the population can increase rapidly, especially if there has been just enough snow cover to shield the lemmings from aerial predation by hawks and owls. These periodic population explosions are a feature of lemming biology and may lead to mass dispersal, when swarms of lemmings migrate, apparently at random, across the tundra.

MOUNTAIN WILDLIFE

9

Predators

The scarcity of plant material in mountain environments limits the *density* of mountain herbivore populations. Sheep and goats, for example, occur at much lower densities than similar species that live in more productive environments, such as the antelopes of the African plains. With such low concentrations of herbivores in the mountains, it is not surprising to find that the predators that rely on these animals as a source of food are also very scarce.

Rare, well camouflaged, nocturnal and superbly adapted to living in a cold, steep environment, the snow leopard is the epitome of a mountain predator. It lives throughout the Himalayas, where it feeds on ibex, blue sheep and marmots, as well as smaller rodents and birds.

Snow leopards are solitary, coming together only during the breeding season. After they have mated, the male leaves the female to rear the cubs on her own.

In the mountains of North and South America the cougar, or mountain lion, is the major predator. It feeds mainly on deer, but will take practically anything, including porcupine, beaver and small mammals. The cougar will not usually finish a carcass immediately, but will cover it with leaves and return for a second meal later.

Many of the smaller cats are found in mountains, normally on the wooded lower slopes rather than the open alpine meadows. Lynx are the most widespread, occurring throughout Europe, Asia and America. They feed on birds and rodents, but have been known to take small deer. In North America their main food is the mountain hare.

The wildcat is found throughout the mountainous areas of Europe, but is a shy animal and is rarely seen. Although similar in size and coloring to the domestic tabby cat, the wildcat has a reputation for being very fierce.

Some species of cat normally associated with tropical climates have adapted to living in the mountains. The leopard is found in many mountains throughout Asia, while the Siberian tiger inhabits the bleak mountain strongholds of eastern Russia. The mountain forms of these species are generally larger than their lowland cousins, an adaptation that improves their ability to conserve heat.

Two members of the dog family are common mountain predators. Wolves hunt, either in packs or alone, across the snowy slopes of many mountain ranges, and the red fox has a similarly broad distribution. Wolves can kill large mammals like caribou and even moose. Like most other carnivores, they tend to take old, sick or young animals rather than healthy adults.

Wolf cubs are born in May but do not start to hunt with the pack until September. Seven cubs is the average litter, though a maximum of twelve has been recorded. Despite this high birth rate, wolves are rare. Like other predators, they take sheep and goats and are, therefore, shot mercilessly by farmers and herdsmen. In many parts of the world people are scared of wolves and may shoot them out of fear, though there is no known record of anyone ever having been killed by one.

Above: a red fox hunts mice in deep snow.

Facing page top: a snow leopard.

Facing page bottom: the bobcat is similar to the lynx. This one is chasing a snowshoe hare.

10
Scavengers

Above: the griffon vulture is supreme among the mountain scavengers.

Left: ravens are ubiquitous scavengers found in most mountainous regions.

Mountains are dangerous places to live. Even the most sure-footed mountain goat can slip and fall on a steep cliff. The harsh winter also produces fatalities as sick or under-weight animals succumb to the chill wind and lack of food and avalanches sweep many ibex to their death.

Many animals include carrion as part of a more general diet. Foxes, for example, will take scraps from carcasses, but also feed on rodents, earthworms and insects. Eagles will occasionally feed on carrion, but prefer to kill their own prey.

The undisputed king of mountain scavengers is the griffon vulture. This is a large, heavily-built bird that nests on cliff ledges and can be seen soaring high among the mountain peaks on the look-out for food.

As the sun warms the cold night air, the griffons leave their roost and flap slowly along the cliffs, searching for the currents of warm air that create thermals. The birds gain height by soaring in the thermals, and spend the day scanning the slopes. Once a carcass has been spotted, the griffons circle over it, making sure that it is safe to land. This is important, as vultures are big birds and cannot take off quickly if attacked. They are especially vulnerable after they have eaten, as thay tend to gorge themselves to the limit and often have to digest some of the meal before they are light enough to fly.

Bald eagles gather round a carcass in winter.

Most vultures tend to eat the soft parts of a carcass like the meat and entrails, but they leave the bones. This prevents them from feeding on the bone marrow, a rich source of protein and fat which is encased inside the bones.

The lammergaier, however, has evolved a highly specialized feeding behavior which allows it to do just this. Once the larger vultures have eaten their fill, the lammergaier carries the bones high into the sky and drops them onto large rocks from such a height that they split open. The bird then swoops down and eats the exposed marrow.

While they feed, the vultures are pestered by other, smaller scavengers. Crows, ravens and magpies are all adept at picking edible scraps from carcasses and can move quickly enough to be able to avoid attack from the vultures.

11
Birds of Prey

Birds of prey represent one of the greatest threats to small birds and mammals in the mountains. From the tiny merlin to the massive golden eagle, these airborne predators have superb eyesight and a dramatic turn of speed.

The peregrine is a medium-sized falcon with a slate-gray back and pale undersides. Its wings are long, curved and pointed and can be folded along its body for improved streamlining when it accelerates. Peregrines fly high, keeping a sharp eye open for potential prey. When a peregrine decides to attack, it folds its wings and "stoops", dropping at speeds of up to 155 mph onto its victim. The violence of the attack can kill birds up to the size of a pigeon.

Once common, the peregrine is now rare, especially in Europe and North America. This is partly because of persecution from gamekeepers (peregrines are partial to gamebirds), but is also due to the use of agricultural pesticides. Being at the top of the food chain, peregrines and other birds of prey concentrate these damaging chemicals in their bodies. The chemicals interfere with egg formation, causing the birds to lay eggs with weak shells, thus reducing the birds' breeding success. The most dangerous chemicals have now been banned and peregrine numbers show some signs of recovery.

Possibly the most spectacular bird of prey in the mountains is the golden eagle. This massive bird nests on tiny cliff ledges and may raise up to two chicks. Whereas peregrines stoop from a great height onto their prey, golden eagles fly low over the slopes, searching for medium-sized prey such as hares, rabbits or marmots. They are remarkably manoeuvrable birds, and can follow the zig-zag movements of a fleeing hare with considerable accuracy.

A similar hunting method is used by the merlin, one of the smaller falcons found on the mountains. The merlin flies fast and low over open moorland, flushing small birds from the shelter of the heather.

Facing page: a buzzard on the look-out for its prey.
Below: peregrine falcons nest on cliff ledges.

12
Bird Diversity

To some birds, mountain ranges are simply barriers that have to be passed as they migrate from winter refuges to their summer breeding grounds. Migrating songbirds fly along the valleys that form natural passageways through the mountains. The valley vegetation provides feeding sites along the way, where the weary travellers can replenish their minimal energy supplies. Larger birds often fly a more direct route and may reach remarkable altitudes as they fly right over a mountain range. Bar-headed geese have even been seen flying over Mount Everest, the highest mountain in the world, as they migrate from the plains of India to their breeding grounds on the Central Asian Plateau.

Compared to the long-distance migrants, the resident mountain gamebirds appear absurdly clumsy. These birds are ground-dwellers, taking to the air only when there is an immediate threat to their safety. Some of the brilliantly colored forest pheasants need to gain a vantage point from which to launch themselves. Once airborne, however, they can glide at considerable speed so long as the gradient of the slope allows them to descend rapidly. They are not so good at level flight.

The gamebirds of the higher slopes, like the snowcock and chukor (a kind of partridge), are more capable fliers, though they rely heavily on their cryptic coloration to protect them from predation. These birds stay at altitude throughout the year, living on seeds and plant shoots.

Many songbirds live in the mountains. Warblers, redstarts, bluebirds and finches may all be found searching for insects or seeds in the high alpine meadows, along stream banks and in the woodlands which cover the lower slopes.

With food in its bill, a mountain bluebird pauses at its nest entrance.

Wheatears are among the smaller birds that spend the summer in the mountains.

The beautifully colored wall-creeper, which is found throughout the mountains of southern Europe and Asia, has adapted to a life on the steep cliffs. It clings tenaciously to vertical rock walls, probing dark crevices with a long, curved bill as it searches for insects. Preferring to live near their food supply, wall-creepers nest in cavities on the cliffs.

One of the most unusual mountain birds is the Andean flamingo. Although flamingos are normally associated with the great lakes of the African plains, this species breeds high in the Andean mountains in Bolivia, finding tiny plants and animals to eat in shallow, brackish lakes. In winter the flamingos migrate southwards along the Andes to southern Chile. There they descend to sea level, where the weather is milder than on the high breeding grounds.

Above: the Himalayan snowcock is one of the largest mountain game birds and relies on its cryptic coloration for protection from predation.

Top: geese are among the highest fliers in the world.

13
Mountain Misfits

Giant pandas are only found in the thick bamboo forests of western China.

A Japanese macaque, or snow monkey, and her young.

Alongside the true mountain animals are a number of species which you would not expect to see on the mountains, like the flamingos in Bolivia, and others that are so unusual that they deserve a special mention. There may even be animals in the mountains that are yet to be discovered!

The giant panda is one of the best-known "mountain misfits". It is a large, bear-like animal that lives in the dense bamboo forests that cover the mountains of western China. This black-and-white giant eats nothing but bamboo shoots, a food source that is becoming increasingly rare as the forests are cleared to make way for farming. Its only close relative is the much smaller red panda, which lives throughout the forested lower slopes of the Himalayas.

Another giant of the mountain world is the wild yak. This enormous creature looks like a huge, shaggy black cow and lives far above the tree line throughout the year. Because it is a bad-tempered beast, the wild yak is feared by local herdsmen. Domestic yaks are much tamer and are used to work and carry loads on farms in Tibet.

In Africa, both the African elephant and the mountain gorilla are found on mountains. There is a famous population of mountain gorillas on the forested slopes of the Virunga Volcanoes in Ruanda. The gorillas feed on leaves, bark and fruit and live in social groups of up to thirty individuals. They often spend the night in a hastily constructed "nest" among the branches of a tree, though they are not terribly agile climbers.

Scientists have been studying the behavior of these gorillas for many years. Because of constant human presence, the gorillas are now used to seeing people in the forest and do not

run away when approached. This makes them relatively easy to watch – but it also means that poachers can get near enough to shoot them. Gorilla heads and feet are sold illegally as souvenirs in local markets, so the gorillas are now in serious danger of being wiped out.

Another primate which has successfully learnt to survive in the mountains is the Japanese macaque. These animals grow a thick coat in winter, which protects them from the severe cold. Sometimes, however, when it becomes particularly cold they crowd into nearby natural, hot springs where they lie soaking in the warm water for hours on end.

In densely forested Virunga National Park, a mountain gorilla feeds on a handful of leaves.

The "Yeti" is probably the most famous mountain mystery. Strange ape-like creatures have been reported in the Himalayas for many years, but scientists have never found one, nor have any photographs been obtained. Outsized footprints found in the Appalachian Mountains of North America suggest the presence of a similar creature, known locally as "Bigfoot", in the New World. These animals remain one of nature's more mysterious secrets.

Glossary

ALTITUDE Height above sea level.

ANTLER A type of horn that is shed and regrown every year.

BURROW A hole in the ground used as a home or shelter by an animal.

CACHE A hidden store of food.

CARNIVORE An animal that only eats meat.

COMPETITION This occurs when two different animals feed on the same food.

CREVASSE A crack in a glacier.

DENSITY The number of animals per unit area.

DORMANT A condition in which little activity takes place.

ENVIRONMENT The surroundings of animals and plants.

FOOD CHAIN A series of organisms in an animal community, each member of which feeds on another in the chain.

GLAND Part of the body which produces a special substance such as sweat, oil or digestive juices.

HABITAT The natural home of an animal or plant.

HERBIVORE An animal that exists on a diet of live plant material.

HIBERNATE (of animals) To enter a dormant phase during the winter.

HORN Hard growth on an animal's head.

KID A young goat.

MONOGAMOUS Of an animal that has only one mate.

MOUNTAIN RANGE A mountainous area which includes many peaks.

RAM An adult male sheep.

RUT The breeding season of sheep, goats and deer.

TREE LINE The upper altitude limit at which trees will grow.

TUNDRA An arctic environment with a ground cover of lichens and mosses.